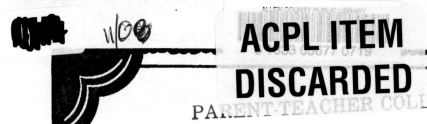
A Guide for Using

Caps for Sale

in the Classroom

Based on the book written by Esphyr Slobodkina

*This guide written by **J. L. Smith***

D1300596

Teacher Created Resources, Inc.
6421 Industry Way
Westminster, CA 92683
www.teachercreated.com

ISBN: 978-1-57690-630-9

©*2000 Teacher Created Resources, Inc.*
Reprinted, 2008
Made in U.S.A.

Edited by
Lorin Klistoff, M.A.

Illustrated by
Ken Tunell

Cover Art by
Wendy Chang

Teacher
Created
Resources

Table of Contents

Introduction

A good book can touch the lives of children like a good friend. The pictures, words, and characters can inspire young minds as they turn to literary treasures for companionship, recreation, comfort, and guidance. Great care has been taken in selecting the books and unit activities that comprise the primary series of Literature Units. Teachers who use this literature unit to supplement their own valuable ideas can plan the activities using one of the following methods.

Sample Lesson Plan

The sample lessons on page 4 provide the teacher with a specific set of lesson plan suggestions. Each of the lessons can take from one to several days to complete and can include all or some of the suggested activities. Refer to the Suggestions for Using the Unit Activities on pages 7–11 for information relating to the unit activities.

Unit Planner

For the teacher who wishes to tailor the suggestions on pages 7–11 in a format other than that prescribed in the Sample Lesson Plan, a blank unit planner is provided on page 5. On a specific day, you may choose the activities you wish to include by writing the activity name or a brief notation about the activity. Space has been provided for reminders, comments, and other pertinent information relating to each day's activities. Reproduce copies of the Unit Planner, as needed.

Sample Lesson Plan

Lesson 1

- Introduce the unit using some or all of the Before the Book activities (page 7).

- Read About the Author (page 6) to the students.

- Introduce the vocabulary and complete one of the vocabulary activities on page 20.

- Complete Examining the Book (page 19).

- Read the story.

Lesson 2

- Read the story for a second time. This may be done as a whole class, individually, or with a partner.

- Prepare the pocket chart (page 12) and use the story questions to involve students in critical thinking (page 16).

- Do Pocket Chart Activities on pages 12 and 13.

- Map the story elements by completing page 21.

- Discuss Career Hats (page 37).

Lesson 3

- Continue discussing story questions (page 16).

- Fill in the summary frame on page 22.

- Discuss rhyming words and complete page 28.

- Complete math problems based on the book (page 31).

- Practice following directions (page 34).

- Label a diagram (page 38).

Lesson 4

- Recall the story sequence (page 23).

- Practice matching contractions (page 24).

- Make a sales poster (page 29).

- Create patterns using caps (page 35).

- Discuss solving problems: What Would You Do? (page 42).

Lesson 5

- Continue discussions based on the book by completing What Do You Think? on page 26.

- Identify characters' actions by completing Who Was It? on page 25.

- Focus on endings to sentences by completing End It Right! on page 27.

- Practice making exact change (page 33).

- Extend learning by completing P. E. Activities on page 45.

Lesson 6

- Make and read the minibook, "Monkeys: A Book of Information" (pages 39–41).

- Complete Barrel of Monkeys activities on page 32.

- Assemble the Monkey Pattern (pages 43 and 44).

- Select a writing activity from page 30.

- Discuss Town and Country (page 36).

Lesson 7

- Choose one (or all) of the culminating activities to conclude the book (pages 46 and 47).

Unit Planner

Unit Activities

Date:

Notes:

Unit Activities

Date:

Notes:

Unit Activities

Date:

Notes:

Unit Activities

Date:

Notes:

Unit Activities

Date:

Notes:

Unit Activities

Date:

Notes:

Getting to Know the Book and the Author

Book Summary

(Available in USA, HarperTrophy, 1940, 1987; Canada, HarperCollins; UK, HarperCollins; AUS, HarperCollins)

Caps for Sale, a much-loved story, tells the tale of what happens to a peddler one day. Each day the peddler walks up and down the street trying to sell caps which he has stacked upon his head. One day when he cannot sell any caps, he decides to take a rest under a tree. When he awakens, he realizes that all of the caps are gone except one. He looks up in the tree to find each hat is now being worn by a monkey. The peddler tries to figure out what to do. Everything that the peddler does, the monkeys copy. Finally, the peddler becomes so frustrated that he takes off his cap and throws it to the ground. The monkeys copy him and throw their caps to the ground, too. The peddler then picks up the caps, stacks them on his head, and begins to sell them again.

About the Author

Esphyr Slobodkina was born in Russia in 1908. The town in which she was born, Chelyabinsk, is at the base of the Ural Mountains in Siberia. She lived and studied art in Manchuria. Esphyr's father worked for the railroads, but as the Russian Revolution began to affect the country, the family fled to several Russian cities.

Finally, the Slobodkina family fled to the United States. In 1935, Esphyr became a United States citizen. She attended school at New York's National Academy of Design and later took design-related jobs such as working as a designer in a textile shop.

A friend introduced Esphyr to famed children's author Margaret Wise Brown. Esphyr provided illustrations for several of Brown's books including *The Little Fireman* (1938), *The Little Farmer* (1948), *The Little Cowboy* (1948), and *Sleepy ABC* (1953). Brown inspired and helped Esphyr start her own career as an author and illustrator.

In addition to *Caps for Sale*, Esphyr has also written and illustrated *The Wonderful Feast* (1955), *Little Dinghy* (Abelard-Schuman, 1958), *Pinky and the Petunias* (Abelard-Schuman, 1959), *The Long Island Ducklings* (Lantern Press, 1961), *Boris and His Balaika* (1964), *Pezzo the Peddler and the Circus Elephant* (Albelard, 1967), and *The Flame, the Breeze, and the Shadow* (1969).

Esphyr is also known as a storyteller, painter, teacher, sculptor, and an amateur architect.

Suggestions for Using the Unit Activities

Use some or all of the following activities to help children understand and appreciate the story, as well as introduce, reinforce, and extend skills across the curriculum. The suggested activities have been divided into three sections to assist the teacher in planning the literature unit.

The sections are as follows:

- *Before the Book* includes suggestions for preparing the classroom environment and the students for the literature to be read.

- *Into the Book* has activities that focus on the book's content, characters, and theme.

- *After the Book* extends the reader's enjoyment of the book.

Before the Book

Complete the following projects before you begin the unit:

- Prepare vocabulary cards, story questions, and sentence strips for the pocket chart activities. (Directions and patterns are provided on pages 12–16.)

- If you do not have access to a commercial pocket chart, make one. The directions for creating your own are on page 12.

- Collect an assortment of books about monkeys to display in the classroom.

- Discuss the vocabulary words with the students. Make copies of the cap or monkey pattern on page 15 on which to write the vocabulary words. Write the definitions on the sentence strips on page 14. Display the vocabulary words and definitions in a pocket chart.

Vocabulary Words				
ordinary	wares	peddler	checked	bunch
cap	disturb	leaned	refreshed	stamped

- Select one of the vocabulary activities on page 20 to reinforce the vocabulary words. Students can create their own vocabulary books by assembling the mini-vocabulary book. On each page, have the students write the vocabulary word and illustrate it. Or try quartering a word. This vocabulary activity requires students to critically think about each vocabulary word.

Suggestions for Using the Unit Activities *(cont.)*

Before the Book *(cont.)*

• Display the book to the students. Have them make predictions telling what the story will be about. Record student predictions on a sheet of butcher paper. Refer back to the predictions after reading the story.

• Allow students time to examine the book. This can be done as a whole class, in small groups, or individually. If students are old enough to complete the task in small groups or independently, have them use Examining the Book (page 19) as a guide.

Into the Book

Language Arts

• **Stick Puppets** (pages 17 and 18)

Have students create stick puppets using the patterns on page 18. A plan for making a theater for the puppets is on page 17. The stick puppets can then be used for many of the language arts activities that follow. For example, use the puppets when conducting discussions based on the critical thinking questions on page 16. Students can also use the puppets while doing their dramatization (page 46).

• **Story Elements** (page 21)

Encourage students to think about the elements that make up a story, specifically the story, *Caps for Sale*. Complete the story map by filling in the setting, characters, problem, and solution. This activity can be completed in a number of ways. Try charting the story map on a large sheet of butcher paper, make a transparency and complete it on the overhead, or reproduce page 21 and have each student work on his or her own copy of the page.

• **Summarize It** (page 22)

Summarize the important events of the story by completing a *Caps for Sale* summary. Page 22 provides a summary frame for students who may need some help organizing their thoughts. For students who do not need the assistance of a frame, provide sentence strips on which they can record the important events. Save the papers from this activity to use with Caps on My Head (page 23).

• **Caps on My Head** (page 23)

This activity combines practice sequencing story events with a fun and cute art project. Copy each sentence from the summary completed in Summarize It (page 22) onto a cap pattern (page 15). Allow students to practice placing the events in the correct order. When the events are correctly placed, glue them together. Then, create the peddler's head by following the directions provided. Glue the stack of caps on top of the peddler's head.

Suggestions for Using the Unit Activities *(cont.)*

Into the Book *(cont.)*

Language Arts *(cont.)*

- **Monkeying Around with Contractions** (page 24)

  An important component of a literature unit is to provide skills practice in conjunction with a piece of literature. Monkeying Around with Contractions provides students the opportunity to match contractions with the words which make the contraction.

- **Who Was It?** (page 25)

  Identifying actions of a character helps develop a sense of character as well as events in the story. While completing Who Was It?, students are asked to determine if it was the peddler or the monkeys who did each event.

- **What Do You Think?** (page 26)

  Monkeys live in tropical forests or grasslands. What were monkeys doing in the country? Ask students to consider these in-depth questions related to the book. Choose to have students fill out this page individually or hold a class discussion.

- **End It Right!** (page 27)

  Provide further skills work by focusing on ending punctuation. End It Right! asks students to determine if the sentences related to the book need to end with a period, exclamation point, or question mark.

- **Rhyming Words** (page 28)

  An important component of the primary grades is learning about rhyming words. Challenge students to think of words which rhyme with each of the words on this page. Each of the words is used in *Caps for Sale*. See if students can find the location of the word in the book.

- **Sales Poster** (page 29)

  Bring several samples of sales advertisements. Discuss the components of each advertisement. Encourage students to think of a sales poster which could be used to sell caps. Use page 29 as a work sheet, then use a larger sheet of construction paper to create the sales poster. Display the posters on a bulletin board.

- **Writing Activities** (page 30)

  Select one, or several, of the writing activities which best suits the needs of your class. Many of these activities can be used in conjunction with the monkey pattern on pages 43 and 44.

Suggestions for Using the Unit Activities *(cont.)*

Into the Book *(cont.)*

Math

- **Figure It Out!** (page 31)

  Challenge students to solve the problems based on the money, caps, monkeys, and peddler in the story.

- **Barrel of Monkeys** (page 32)

  A variety of activities are provided on this page for use with the children's toy, Barrel of Monkeys. Select activities which are appropriate for the age level of children with whom you are working.

- **Exact Change** (page 33)

  Experience and practice making change is an important life skill. Use page 33, Exact Change, to have students practice different coin combinations which equal fifty cents. Extend the idea by having students think of other amounts for which they can practice making change.

- **Following Directions** (page 34)

  Help the peddler find his caps by having students follow directions. Forward, backward, side to side, students will enjoy reuniting the peddler with his caps.

- **Cap Patterns** (page 35)

  Use this page to have students practice identifying and extending patterns.

Social Studies

- **Town and Country** (page 36)

  The setting of *Caps for Sale* changes when the peddler walks out of the town and into the country. Use the change of setting as a way to bring students' attention to the similarities and differences between town and country. If possible, read *Town Mouse Country Mouse* by Jan Brett (Putnam Publishing Group, 1944) and discuss their differences. Page 36 provides students with a place to express what they have learned about the similarities and differences.

- **Career Hats** (page 37)

  This page provides an excellent connection to community workers. Students are asked to match each community worker to the hat he or she would wear.

Science

- **Labeling a Diagram** (page 38)

  Connect *Caps for Sale* to your science curriculum with the use of this page which asks students to label a diagram of the parts of a tree. If this page is too simple for the students with whom you are working, have them create their own diagram and label it.

- **Monkey Book** (pages 39–41)

  Encourage students to learn more about monkeys by assembling and reading this minibook about monkeys. Cut along the dashed lines and staple the pages in order.

Suggestions for Using the Unit Activities *(cont.)*

Into the Book *(cont.)*

Health

- **What Would You Do?** (page 42)

  In the story, the monkeys took something that didn't belong to them. Use this problem from the book as an opportunity to discuss similar problems that students encounter. Provide the steps listed on page 42 as a way for students to solve their problems. Be sure to provide practice with the scenarios listed at the bottom of the page.

Art

- **Monkey Pattern** (pages 43 and 44)

  The monkey pattern provided on pages 43 and 44 is a simple art project that even very young children can do. Cut out the pattern and assemble the pieces by matching the letters. For older students, extend the project by having them attach (or glue) two monkeys together and stuff it with cotton. The result is an adorable 3-D monkey.

Physical Education

- **P. E. Activities** (page 45)

  Several activities are provided which connect *Caps for Sale* with your physical education curriculum. Use them during regularly scheduled P. E. time or as a "break" from the classroom.

After the Book

- **Culminating Activities** (pages 46 and 47)

  Culminate your unit on *Caps for Sale* by selecting one or more of the culminating activities provided on pages 46 and 47. Have students record a dramatic reading of the story onto a cassette. The students can also plan a dramatic play or a big sale of various items.

Pocket Chart Activities

Prepare a pocket chart for storing and using vocabulary cards, question cards, and sentence strips.

How to Make a Pocket Chart

If a commercial pocket chart is unavailable, you can make a pocket chart if you have access to a laminator. Begin by laminating a 24" x 36" (61 cm x 91 cm) piece of colored tagboard. Cut nine 2" x 20" (5 cm x 51 cm) or six 3" x 20" (8 cm x 51 cm) strips of clear plastic to use as pockets. Space the strips equally down the 36" (91 cm) length of the tagboard. Attach each strip with clear, plastic tape along the sides and bottom. This will hold the sentence strips, word cards, etc., and can be displayed in a learning center or mounted on a chalk rail for use with a group.

How to Use a Pocket Chart

1. On brown, light brown, or tan paper, reproduce the monkey pattern on page 15. Copy each vocabulary word found on page 7 on a monkey. Write the corresponding definition for each word on a sentence strip. (Sentence strips are provided on page 14.) Have students match each vocabulary word to the correct definition. When a match has been made, place the vocabulary word and the sentence strip next to each other in the pocket chart. (See illustration below.)

2. Select sentences from the story in which the vocabulary words are used and write them on sentence strips. Display the sentence strips in the pocket chart. Have students think of synonyms for each vocabulary word. Write each synonym on an index card and insert it in the pocket chart covering up the original vocabulary word. Reread each sentence using the synonym in place of the vocabulary word. For an extension, challenge your students to think of an antonym for as many vocabulary words as possible.

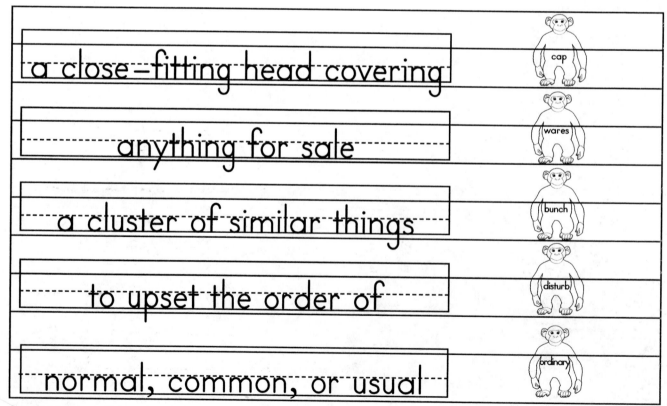

Pocket Chart Activities *(cont.)*

How to Use a Pocket Chart *(cont.)*

3. Summarize the story in several sentences. This can either be done in advance by the teacher or by the students (page 22). Write each sentence on a sentence strip. Each student can then work alone or with a partner at a learning center to practice sequencing the sentence strips. As an extension, have students create their own minibooks by copying the sentences on sheets of paper stapled together. They can then illustrate each page.

4. Reproduce several copies of the cap pattern on page 15 in six different colors. Write a story question from page 16 on each cap pattern. The level of the question can be written on the cap, too. If you desire, laminate each piece for durability. Use a different color of paper for each level of Bloom's Levels of Learning.

   I. Knowledge (*red*)

   II. Comprehension (*orange*)

   III. Application (*yellow*)

   IV. Analysis (*green*)

   V. Synthesis (*blue*)

   VI. Evaluation (*purple*)

I. Knowledge
What was the peddler selling?

After reading the story, use story questions to provide opportunities for students to develop and practice higher-level, critical-thinking skills. Divide the class into teams. Ask for a response to a question from one of the question cards. Teams score a point for each appropriate response.

Work together as a class or small group to write the answer to each question on a sentence strip. As an alternative, students can work on each question by themselves or with a partner.

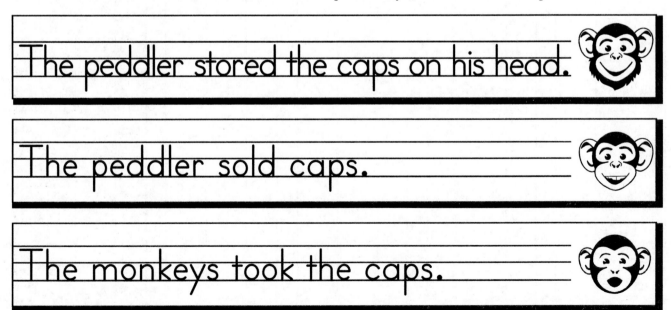

The peddler stored the caps on his head.

The peddler sold caps.

The monkeys took the caps.

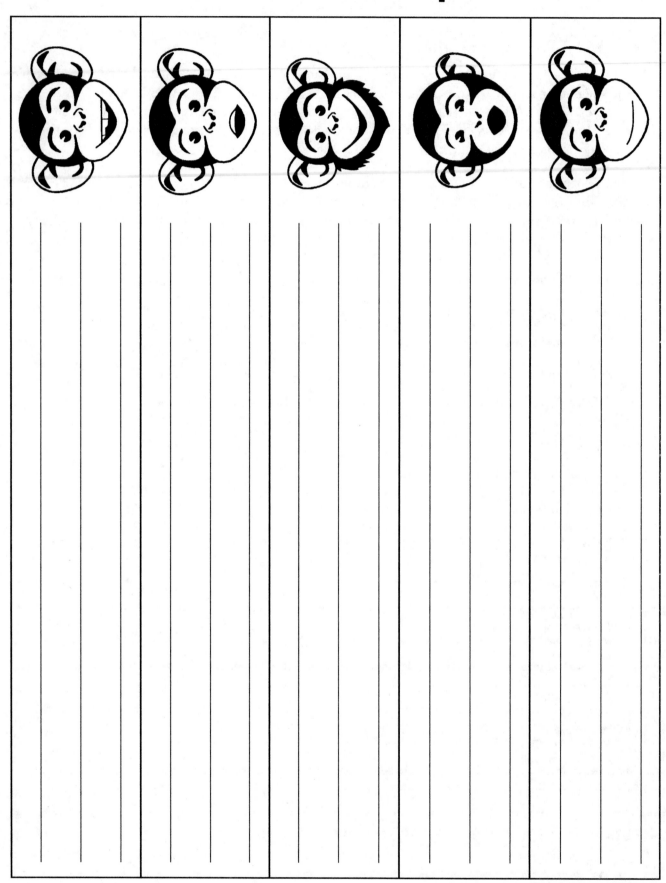

Sentence Strips

Pocket Chart Patterns

Directions: Duplicate these patterns, as needed, for use with the pocket chart activities on pages 12 and 13. Enlarge or reproduce the pattern to fit a particular activity.

Story Questions

Use the following questions based on Bloom's Levels of Learning to develop higher-level, critical thinking skills. The questions promote discussion and provide excellent reasons for returning to the text to review the story.

Reproduce the cap pattern on page 15 and write a different question on each cap. If desired, color code the various level questions. For example, all of the knowledge questions could be written on a cap pattern which has been copied on red paper.

I. Knowledge *(ability to recall learned information)*

- What was the peddler selling?

- Where did the peddler store the caps?

- Who took the caps away from the peddler?

II. Comprehension *(ability to master basic understanding of information)*

- Why didn't the peddler notice when his caps were taken? What was he doing?

- How did the peddler get his caps back?

- What did the peddler do when he got his caps back?

III. Application *(ability to do something new with information)*

- Why did the peddler need his caps back?

- What else could the peddler have done to get the caps back?

- Do you think the peddler will sell caps tomorrow?

IV. Analysis *(ability to examine the parts of a whole)*

- Which cap was the most popular cap? What sentence in the story tells you this?

- What actions of the peddler showed that he was frustrated?

- Why do you think the monkeys were copying the peddler?

V. Synthesis *(ability to bring together information to make something new)*

- Do you think the peddler will take a nap again?

- What could the peddler do to get people to buy his caps?

- How would the story have been different if the peddler would not have taken a nap?

VI. Evaluation *(ability to form and defend an opinion)*

- Look closely at the setting. Would you expect monkeys to live in this environment? Why or why not?

- Why do you think the monkeys took the caps?

- Do you think the peddler likes monkeys? Why or why not?

Stick Puppet Theaters

Make a class set of puppet theaters (one for each student), or make one theater for every two to four students. The patterns and directions for making the stick puppets are on page 18.

Materials

- 22" x 28" (56 cm x 71 cm) piece of colored poster board per theater
- markers, crayons, or paints
- scissors or a craft knife

Directions

1. Fold the poster board 8" (20 cm) in from each of the shorter sides. (See picture below.)
2. Cut a window in the front panel, large enough to accommodate two or three stick puppets.
3. Let the children personalize their own theaters using the markers, crayons, or paint.
4. Laminate the stick puppet theaters to make them more durable. You may wish to send the theaters home at the end of the year or save them to use year after year.

Suggestions for Using the Puppets and the Puppet Theaters

- Prepare the stick puppets. Use the puppets and the puppet theater with a reader's theater script developed from the story.
- Students can practice retelling the story using their own words or by reading the book.
- Use the stick puppets when asking the questions on page 16. Students can hold up the stick puppets to answer the questions. Be sure they hold up the character to whom the question relates.
- Have students continue the story by using the puppets to tell about the next time the peddler takes a nap.

Stick Puppet Patterns

Directions: Reproduce the patterns on this page on tagboard or construction paper. Have students color the patterns. Cut them out along the dashed lines. If desired, laminate the figures for durability. To complete the stick puppets, glue each pattern to a tongue depressor or craft stick. Use the stick puppets with puppet theaters and/or a reader's theater script.

Examining the Book

Directions: Becoming familiar with the features of books is an important part of reading. Explore the features of *Caps for Sale* before you begin reading the story. Use the questions below to examine the book.

1. Look at the cover of the book. What is the title of the book? _____

_____

2. What is the author's name? _____

3. What is illustrated on the cover of the book? _____

_____

4. Based on the title and the cover illustration, what do you think this book will be about? _____

_____

5. Look at the back cover of the book. What information does the back cover provide? _____

_____

6. What is the ISBN number of the book? _____

7. For what do you think the ISBN number is used? _____

_____

8. Turn to the title page of the book. What is the title listed on the title page?

_____

   How is this title different from the title on the cover?_____

_____

9. Does the subtitle listed on the title page change your prediction of what the book will be about? _____

10. What company is the publisher of this book? _____

11. What are the copyright dates on this book? _____

12. To whom is this book dedicated?_____

Vocabulary

Understanding vocabulary used in a story can be essential to a better, deeper understanding of a story. Listed below are words with which your students may not be familiar.

ordinary	peddler	bunch	disturb	refreshed
wares	checked	cap	leaned	stamped

Use the following activities to help your students develop a better understanding of the story words. You may use all of the words listed above or choose to eliminate words your students know. You may even choose to add some of your own from the book.

Mini-Vocabulary Book

Create individual vocabulary books by following the directions below. Then, have students write one word on each page and illustrate the definition of the word. You may wish to have older students write the definition and/or a sentence using the word.

1. Fold an 8.5" x 11" (22 cm x 28 cm) sheet of white paper into eight sections.
2. Cut or tear along the center crease from the folded edge to the next fold line. (See diagram.)
3. Open the paper and push the end sections together.
4. Fold into a little book.

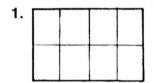

cut slit to here

Quarter a Word

Choose a few words to "quarter" together as a class or assign groups of students one or two words to "quarter." When the groups are done, they can report back to the rest of the class with their findings.

Students can either fold a piece of paper into four sections or draw a rectangle or square and divide that into four sections. In the first section, write the vocabulary word. In the second section, write a definition of the word. The definition can either be looked up in the dictionary or defined by the students. The third section contains a picture of the word. The picture can either be drawn or cut out of an old magazine. The final section includes a sentence which demonstrates how the word is used.

Vocabulary Word	Definition
cap	An unusually soft and close–fitting head covering, either brimless or with a visor.
Picture	**Sentence**
	The peddler sold caps.

Story Elements

Directions: Using a story map is an excellent way of looking at the structure of a story. A story map is simply a visual representation of the elements that make up a story: title, setting, characters, problem, and solution. Use the story map below to take a closer look at the elements that make up the story, *Caps for Sale*.

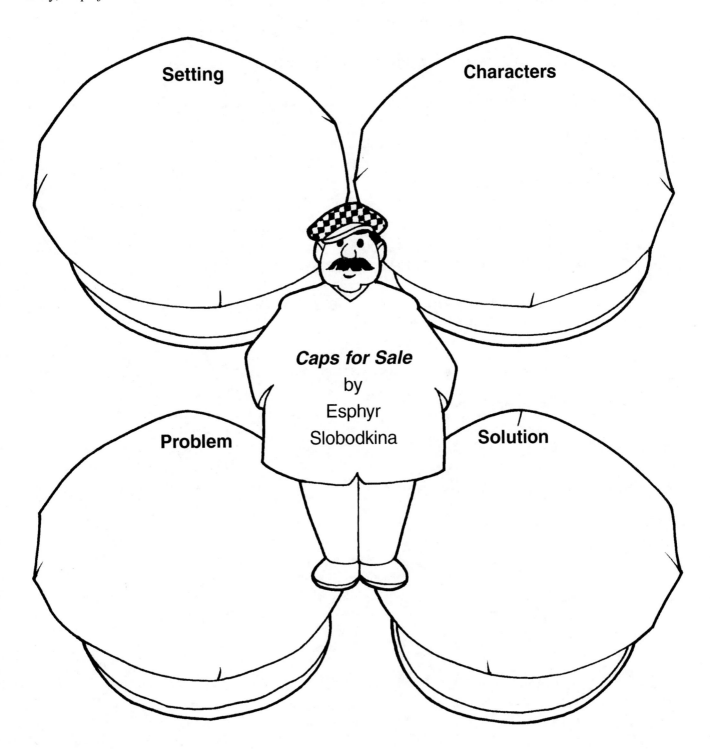

Setting

Characters

Caps for Sale
by
Esphyr
Slobodkina

Problem

Solution

Summarize It

A *summary* is a shortened retelling of a story. In a summary, only the main parts of the story are included. Important events are included in a summary, but details are left out. Being able to summarize a story shows that you understand the story. Use the frame below to help you summarize the story, *Caps for Sale*. Then, use your summary to complete the sequencing project on page 23.

Caps for Sale Summary

1. Once there was a peddler selling _____.

2. One day, he _____.

3. So he _____.

4. When he woke up, _____.

5. He looked up in the tree and saw _____.

6. The peddler didn't know what to do. He shook his _____, shook his _____, and stomped his _____.

7. The monkeys _____.

8. Finally, the peddler _____.

9. The monkeys _____.

10. The peddler picked up the caps and _____.

Caps on My Head

Use the summary from page 22 to complete this activity, which can be adapted to suit the age level of your students. For younger students, have the important events already written out on sentence strips. Practice sequencing the sentence strips before asking them to work on the project below.

Rewrite the sentences summarizing the events of *Caps for Sale* onto copies of a cap (pattern on page 15). Copy one sentence onto each cap. Have each student work with a partner to practice sequencing the events in the correct order. When the caps are in the correct order, follow the directions below for creating a head for the peddler. Then, glue the caps on the peddler's head in sequential order. The result is a delightful project which students can use to practice retelling the story. Younger students who may not be able to read the book yet will be able to read this version.

Making the Peddler's Head

Materials (per student)

- 9" x 12" (23 cm x 30 cm) sheet of peach construction paper

- 8.5" x 3.25" (21.5 cm x 8.5 cm) sheet of black construction paper

- black crayon or marker

Directions

1. Round each of the corners on the sheet of peach construction paper.

2. Fold the piece of 8.5" x 3.25" (21.5 cm x 8.5 cm) sheet of black construction paper in half widthwise. (See illustration.)

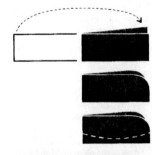

3. Working with the side which has an opening (the non-folded side), round one of the corners. (See illustration.)

4. Round the other corner and bottom. (See illustration.)

5. Glue the larger piece of black paper to the 9" (23 cm) side of the peach paper forming the hair.

6. Glue the remaining piece of black paper on the face to use as the man's mustache.

7. Use a black crayon or marker to draw eyes, eyebrows, a nose, and a mouth on the face. Look at the illustrations in the book for ideas. They do not have to be elaborate.

Monkeying Around with Contractions

There are several contractions used in the story, *Caps for Sale*. A *contraction* is a way of shortening a word or words by leaving out some letters. People use contractions all the time when speaking. Knowing the words used to form the contraction is important. Match the following words to their contractions by drawing a line from the monkey to the tree.

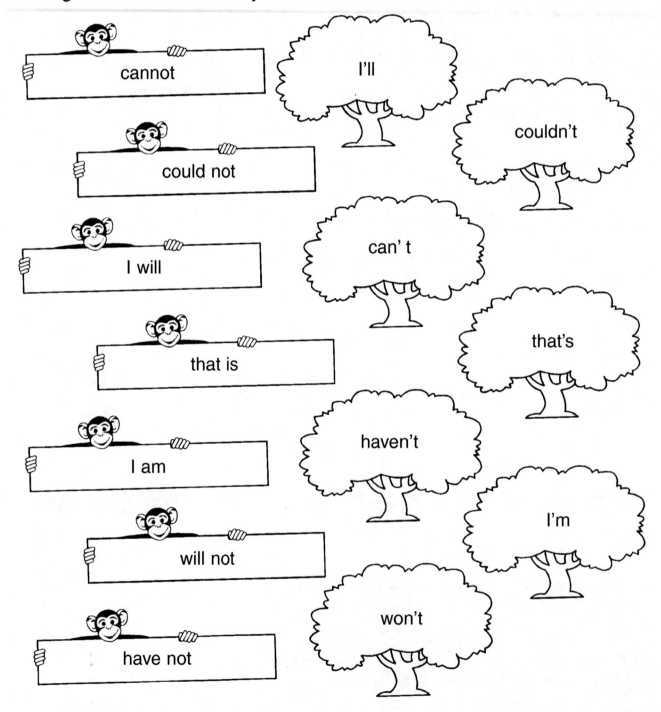

Who Was It?

Read over the events from the story below. Decide whether the monkeys or the peddler did the action. Cut out and glue the correct word in the box in each sentence. Refer back to the book if you need to refresh your memory.

1. The [　] walked down the streets selling caps.

2. The [　] took a nap next to a tree in the country.

3. The [　] took the caps while the peddler was sleeping.

4. The [　] became mad when he discovered his caps were gone.

5. The [　] shook his hands and stamped his feet.

6. The [　] copied everything the peddler did.

7. The [　] threw his own cap on the ground.

8. The [　] copied the peddler and threw their caps, too.

| peddler | peddler | peddler | peddler |
| monkeys | monkeys | monkeys | peddler |

What Do You Think?

Take a moment to think about the following questions. If you need to, discuss them in a small group. Then, write down what you think about the following questions.

The peddler wore all of the same colored caps together. Why do you think he did this?

_____

_____

_____

Monkeys live in tropical forests or grasslands. What were monkeys doing in the country?

_____

_____

_____

The monkeys took all of the caps but the checkered cap. Why didn't the monkeys take the peddler's checkered cap?

_____

_____

_____

The monkeys gave the caps back when the peddler threw his down. If they had not given the caps back, what else do you think the peddler could have done?

_____

_____

_____

End It Right!

Read the following sentences. Decide if each one needs a period, exclamation point, or question mark. Write the correct punctuation mark at the end of the sentence.

1. Caps! Caps for sale! Fifty cents a cap _____

2. The peddler went for a walk in the country _____

3. The peddler fell asleep under a tree _____

4. All the peddler felt was his own checkered cap _____

5. The peddler looked all around _____

6. What do you think the peddler saw _____

7. Monkeys, give me back my caps _____

8. The peddler shook his hands and stamped his feet _____

9. The monkeys took off the caps and threw them down on the ground _____

10. The peddler picked them up and went back into town _____

Now, write your own sentences which end with a period, exclamation point, and question mark. See if you can have them relate to the story, *Caps for Sale.*

Period _____

Exclamation Point _____

Question Mark_____

Rhyming Words

Words which rhyme end with the same sound or sounds. Take a look at the words from the book listed below. Can you think of some words which rhyme with these words? Write them on the lines below.

cap	top	like
_____ _____ _____	_____ _____ _____	_____ _____ _____
blue	**town**	**not**
_____ _____ _____	_____ _____ _____	_____ _____ _____
red	**rest**	**tree**
_____ _____ _____	_____ _____ _____	_____ _____ _____
sleep	**time**	**hand**
_____ _____ _____	_____ _____ _____	_____ _____ _____

Extension: Find some more words in the book for which you can think of rhyming words. Write the word from the book on the back of this paper and the rhyming words underneath.

Sales Poster

In *Caps for Sale*, the peddler tried to sell his caps. Create a sales poster for something that you would like to sell. Use this page as a pre-writing activity to help you think about what might be on the poster.

Materials

- 12" x 18" (30 cm x 46 cm) sheet of white construction paper
- markers, crayons, or paints
- a copy of this work sheet

Item for sale _____   Cost _____

Where can this item be purchased?_____

Are there dates between which the sale will take place?_____

_____

Is there any additional information (sizes, colors, shapes, etc.) which you will want to advertise?_____

_____

Before beginning your poster, briefly sketch out what you want your poster to look like below. Then use this sketch as a guide when you draw your poster.

Writing Activities

Write an Innovation

Use the premise for *Caps for Sale* to create students' own version of the story. Have students consider changing one or more of the following in their new version:

- Change the main character (the peddler).

- Change the item that the peddler sold.

- Change the animal that takes the caps.

- Change the way in which the peddler gets the caps back.

This activity may be done in a variety of ways. Try it as a whole class, a cooperative group, or individually.

Write a Friendly Letter

Ask the students, "What would you do if someone had something of yours and would not give it back?" Have students write a friendly letter to the peddler telling him a different way to solve his problem.

Invent a Display Case

The peddler carried and displayed the caps he was trying to sell on his head. Have students think of another way the peddler could have carried and displayed the caps. This new way of carrying the caps can already exist or they can invent their own. Have them write a description of the new display case. Be sure to include a picture!

A New Call

The peddler walked up and down the streets calling, "Caps! Caps for sale! Fifty cents a cap!" Have students write a new phrase for the peddler to call out. Remember, it has to be something that will encourage people to buy caps.

Busy Townspeople

The day that this story takes place, nobody wants to buy a cap, not even a red cap. There are not even any other people on the streets of the town to buy a cap. Have the students write a story about the other people in the town. Where are they and what are they doing? Why is it that they don't want to buy a cap from the peddler today?

Monkey Business

Monkeys are often associated with trouble. Have the students write another story with monkeys as characters. What do the monkeys do to get into trouble this time? How is the problem solved?

Figure It Out!

You will find five math problems to solve on this page. Before you begin your problem solving, answer questions 1–4. Knowing these answers will help you do your math for questions 5–9.

1. How many caps did the peddler have on his head? _____

2. How many caps did he have on his head that were for sale? _____

3. How many caps of each color did the peddler have to sell?

_____ gray _____ brown _____ blue _____ red

4. How much money did the peddler charge for a cap? _____

5. If the peddler sold 4 red caps, how many red caps would he have left?

_____ red caps

6. How many caps would the peddler sell if he sold all his gray and brown caps?

_____ caps

7. If the peddler sold half of the caps he had to sell, how many caps would he have left to sell?

_____ caps

8. If the peddler sold all the caps except his own, how many caps would he sell?

_____ caps

9. How much money would the peddler make if he sold all the caps he had to sell? (Remember, the checkered cap was his and not for sale!)

Answer: _____

Extension: Turn this paper over and write some of your own story problems based on *Caps for Sale* and the information you compiled at the top of this page.

Barrel of Monkeys

Purchase the toy, Barrel of Monkeys. This toy can still be found in the toy department of stores such as Target or K-Mart. Use Barrel of Monkeys for the activities listed below. If you do not have access to the toy, reproduce the monkey pattern on page 15 in various colors (red, blue, green, and yellow). These paper patterns can still be used to do the activities.

Estimating

Place all of the monkeys from the barrel into a see-through container. Set the container, sticky notes, and a pencil on a table. Encourage students to estimate how many monkeys are in the container. Leave one monkey out on the table as a reference. Create a sign which says, "This is one monkey. Estimate how many monkeys are in the container. Write your name and your answer on the sticky note." Then, with the students, compare the answer to the estimates.

Sort by Color

If reading this book with very young children, use the various color monkeys as a sorting activity. Practice sorting the monkeys into groups by color. First, do the activity with the children. Then, see if they can do it by themselves.

Monkey Patterns

Use the monkeys to create color patterns. Start out with a simple pattern such as green, red, green, red (ABAB). Then move into more complicated patterns with all four colors. See if your students can use the monkeys to create other patterns such as AB, AAB, ABB, AABB, ABC, and ABCD.

Encourage students to create their own patterns using the monkeys. Some students may get very creative and create patterns such as AABCD.

Measuring

Because the monkeys are all the same size and shape, they can be used as a non-standard unit of measurement. Link the monkeys together to create a measuring tool. Ask students to measure various items in the classroom (such as the height of a desk, etc.) with their new measuring tool. Students will have fun measuring with this string of monkeys.

Exact Change

"Caps! Caps for sale! Fifty cents a cap!" was the call of the peddler. But there are many ways to make fifty cents. Look at the example below and then see if you can come up with a few other ways to make fifty cents. Circle coins in each row to equal fifty cents. (*Note*: The coins do not need to be next to each other.)

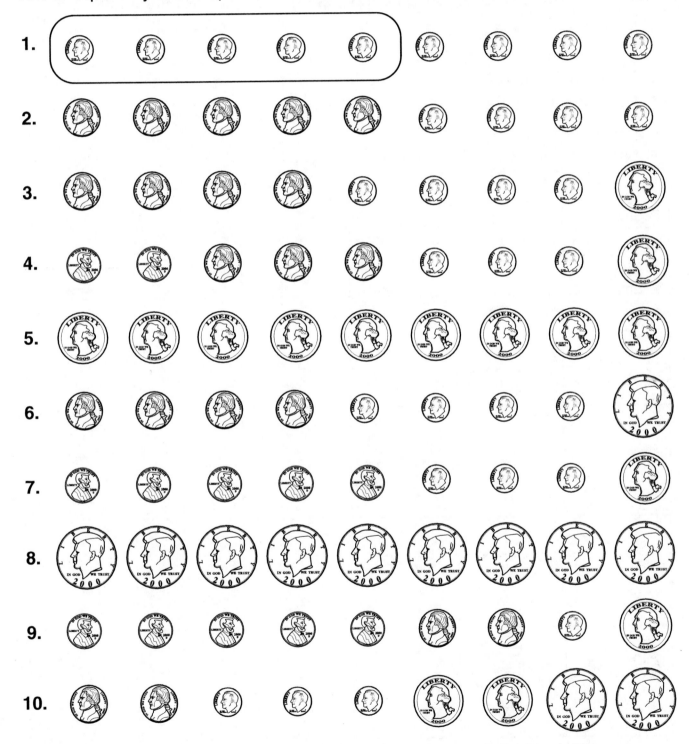

Extension: See how many coin combinations you can make for a different amount. Try seventy-five cents!

Following Directions

When the peddler woke up and could not find his caps, he looked to the right of him, to the left of him, in back of him, and behind the tree. Start at the peddler box and then follow the directions to help the peddler find his caps. When you have reached the last direction, glue the picture of the caps in the square.

1. Move up 3 squares.
2. Move to the right 4 squares.
3. Move up 1 square.
4. Move to the left 1 square.
5. Move down 2 squares.
6. Move up 1 square. Glue the caps in this square.

Cap Patterns

The peddler wore the caps on his head with each color grouped together. There are other ways to organize the caps though. Use the colors of the caps—gray, brown, blue, and red—to color the caps below. Once you have colored each of the caps labeled, see if you can extend the pattern. What would come next?

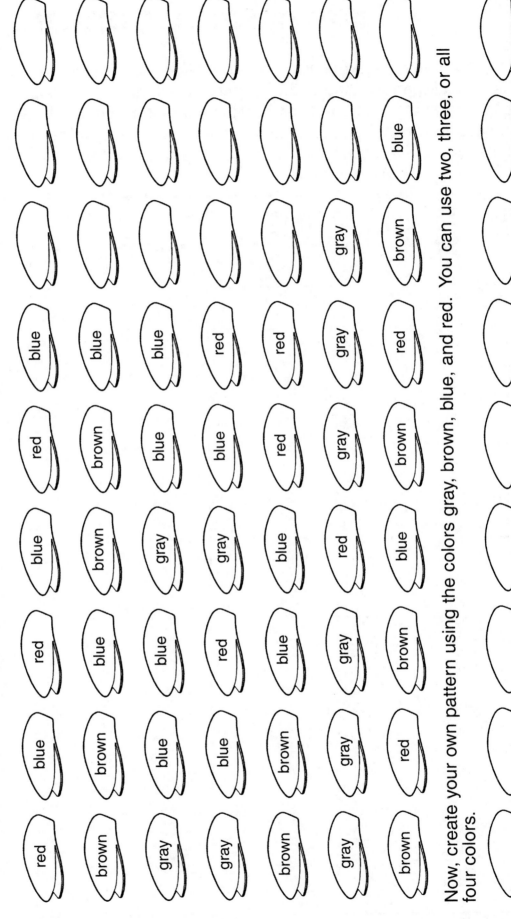

Now, create your own pattern using the colors gray, brown, blue, and red. You can use two, three, or all four colors.

Town and Country

The setting of the story (where the story takes place) changes as the peddler walks out of the town and to the country. Think about the differences between the town and the country. Then complete the chart below. Write words or phrases, draw pictures, or cut out pictures from a magazine to show the differences and the similarities between the town and the country.

 **Town**	 **Country**

Career Hats

The kind of hat a person wears often tells us about that person's career. See if you can figure out which person belongs to each hat. Draw a line from the hat to the person who wears it. Then, on the back of the paper, write a story about one of the people.

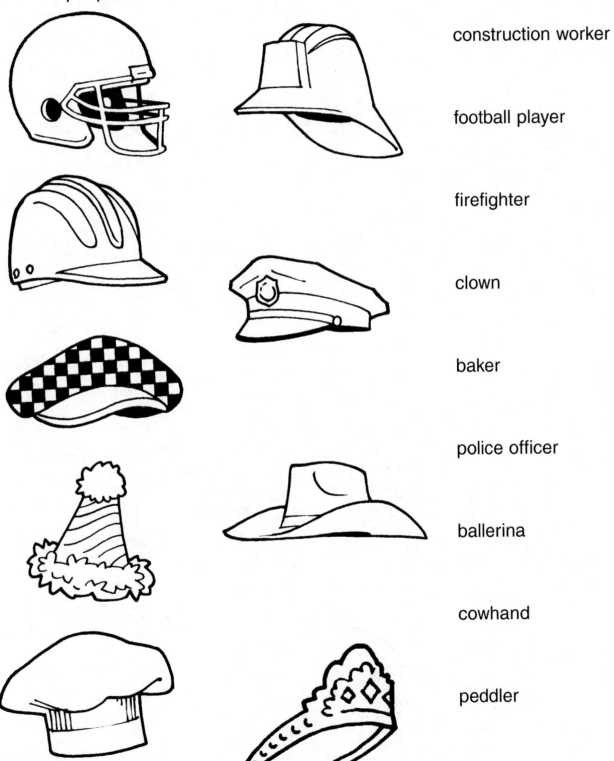

construction worker

football player

firefighter

clown

baker

police officer

ballerina

cowhand

peddler

Labeling a Diagram

The peddler sat under a tree, leaned against the trunk, and fell asleep. Do you know what the different parts of a tree are called? Write each word below in the correct box. Then write the function of each part on the back of this paper. For example, the job or function of the roots is to get food and water to the tree.

trunk   **soil**   **branches**   **leaves**   **roots**

Monkey Book

Directions: Learn more about monkeys by cutting out, assembling, and reading this minibook.

Monkeys:

A Book of Information

Name _____

1

Old World   **New World**

There are more than 100 types of monkeys. They are divided into two groups, Old World monkeys and New World monkeys. The Old World monkeys live in Africa and Southeast Asia. The New World monkeys live in South America and Central America. A monkey can live to be more than 20 years old.

2

Monkey Book *(cont.)*

Monkeys live in tropical forests or grasslands. They eat leaves, grass, insects, fruits, and nuts.

3

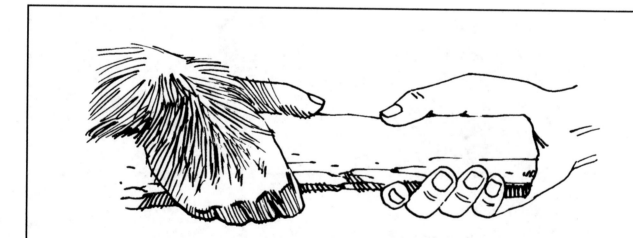

Monkeys have thumbs just like you. A monkey's thumb helps him hold onto and climb trees. Many types of monkeys also use their tails to help them hold the branches of trees.

4

Monkey Book *(cont.)*

Many types of monkeys live together in groups called troops. Monkeys live in a troop for protection and companionship. Monkeys do many things together with their troop. One of the most important activities they do together is grooming.

5

A baby monkey stays close to his or her mother by clinging to her back. The mother monkey does everything she normally does, climb, jump, hang, and groom, even with the baby on her back.

6

What Would You Do?

In *Caps for Sale*, the peddler became very frustrated and angry when the monkeys would not give the caps back to him. On the back of this page, list the things that he did to try to get the caps back.

What do you think the peddler should have done in order to get his caps back? Has someone ever taken something from you and would not give it back? What did you do to get it back?

There are three simple steps you can follow in order to solve problems with other people. Read through these steps, and then see if you can put them into practice.

Problem-Solving Steps

1. Try talking to him or her. Rather than tattling, try talking to the person with whom you have a problem. Begin your sentence with "I don't like it when . . ." By stating your problem this way, you are saying how you feel rather than accusing.

2. If talking to the person does not work, try walking away from the problem. If someone is teasing you, move away from that person. If your friend is not playing a game by the rules and will not listen to you when you try explaining the problem, now is not a good time to play with him or her. Find something else to do.

3. Tell an adult if the person follows you and continues with the problem. If you have followed the first two steps, you have done everything you can to solve the problem. If the problem continues, get an adult involved to help you solve the problem. A good way to get an adult's help is to explain the problem and what you have done to solve the problem.

Following the steps listed above can be a great way to solve your own problems. Can you think of any circumstances when following these steps would not be a good idea? What about if someone is hurt or in danger? Do you want to take the time to go through these three steps, or would you rather get help from an adult immediately?

Now, see if you can use the problem-solving steps above to help solve these problems. Work in a small group to discuss what you would do in the following situations.

- You are playing four square and Marco is not playing by the school rules. He is making up his own rules. What would you do?

- Jenny will not get off the swing after you have waited patiently for your turn. What would you do?

- Max has taken your eraser and is using it as his own. What would you do?

- Julia has fallen off of the slide on the playground. She has a cut on her knee which is bleeding. What would you do?

Monkey Pattern

Directions: Color, cut out, and glue together, matching the letters.

Monkey Pattern *(cont.)*

P. E. Activities

Use these activities to extend your reading of *Caps for Sale* to your physical education activities.

Monkey See, Monkey Do

In this game, one person (or team) is the peddler and the rest of the class (or the other team) are the monkeys. The peddler must come up with an action or activity which the monkeys then must copy. The action can be as simple as hopping in place or as complicated as a pattern such as a hop, two jumping jacks, and three push ups.

If playing the game with two teams, give the team which is the peddler, an opportunity to coordinate which actions they will perform. Be sure to give each person a chance to be the peddler and a monkey.

Good Posture

In the story, the peddler had to hold himself very straight so that the caps would not fall off his head. Explain to your students the reasons that the peddler had to walk so straight. Share with your students the importance of having good posture and then work with them on good posture. This can be done by practicing walking holding their heads up. Try placing a book on the tops of their heads. Can they walk while balancing the book on their heads? Practice good posture while sitting in a chair, too.

The Peddler Jive

Anyone can do the Peddler Jive by following the simple steps the peddler did while trying to get his caps back. Find a fun piece of music which is not too fast. Then simply follow the steps below by doing each action four times in a row to the beat.

1. Shake your finger (pointer finger) on your right hand.

2. Shake your finger (pointer finger) on your left hand.

3. Shake your fingers (pointer fingers) on both hands.

4. Make a fist and shake your right hand.

5. Make a fist and shake your left hand.

6. Make fists and shake both hands.

7. Stamp your right foot.

8. Stamp your left foot.

9. Stamp both feet together and shout.

10. Repeat these movements until the music ends.

Remind the students that the peddler was frustrated and wanted his caps back. See if they can practice making facial expressions which would go with the dance movements. Have fun dancing!

Culminating Activities

Use one of the activities on this page or page 47 as a culminating experience.

Dramatic Reading

A dramatic reading, which is recorded onto a cassette, is an excellent keepsake for students capable of reading the story. When read with expression, this story lends itself to a lot of drama and suspense. Have your students practice reading the story with voice variation and expression.

Arrange a time for each student to do his or her own dramatic reading onto a tape. An excellent way to manage this is to have a parent help by taking one student at a time to a corner of the room to record the dramatic reading. The parent can run the tape recorder so that all the student has to worry about is reading. When the students are finished, have them decorate their own cassette jackets containing the following information: name of the story, author of the story, who is doing the dramatic reading, and the date.

There are several ways to cover the cost of the tapes. Donations are always a great, free way to reduce costs. Contact local music stores to see if they make donations to schools. If you make the need known to parents, they will often send one (or more) blank tapes to school. If you want to coordinate purchasing the cassettes, ask for a donation from each student to cover costs of the tapes. If costs are too prohibitive to have a cassette for each student, perform the dramatic reading for another group of students. Pair each of your students with a child from another class and have your students read the story aloud. This is an excellent way to share a story!

Dramatization

Dramatizing the story is fun for students of all ages and provides an excellent way for students who cannot read the story themselves to share the book with others. In dramatizing the story, the teacher (or a capable reader) is the narrator. The narrator tells the entire story. The actors do not speak; they only act out what the narrator is saying. Select one student (or several) to be the peddler. The rest of the children can be monkeys. As the narrator reads the story out loud, the children act out the story.

Provide several opportunities for your students to practice acting out their parts. Props are not necessary; however, they do add to the production. If caps such as those shown in the pictures are too hard to come by, use baseball caps. When you are ready, invite another class to come and enjoy the story with you.

Culminating Activities *(cont.)*

═══════════════════ **A Sale of Your Own** ═══════════════════

Provide your students with the experience of being peddlers. (**Note:** Before you begin, check your school or district policy to see if this activity is permitted.) Decide, as a class, something that you could sell at your school. Your item could be lemonade, friendship bracelets, pictures that your students draw, or something your students dream up. After you have decided what you will sell, you will need to decide when and where the sale will take place. This can be as simple as students walking around on the playground at recess or setting up a table on which items can be displayed right outside your classroom door.

Have your students help determine how you will advertise your items for sale. Will you call out the price as the peddler did? If you do call out the price, what will your saying be? Will you create flyers and distribute them at recess? Will you have signs that you hang around the school?

The final step is to have the sale. Encourage students to help set up the day of the sale and carry out all of the responsibilities of holding a sale. Where will they keep the money? Who will do the selling? What will they do if they run out of an item? What will they do with the money? These are all things that they will need to consider. Above all, have fun. This is a wonderful learning experience for students and an excellent way to make a connection to the book.

An excellent way to extend this activity is to invite another class to the sale, rather than having it publicly. In advance, provide the students in the other class with "peddler cash" which they can redeem for the items being sold by your class. In this way, each student from the other class can purchase something. Allow your students to redeem the peddler cash by purchasing a popcorn party from you. Or, allow the class to determine how the money will be split among the students. Individual students can then redeem the peddler cash for items such as stickers, pencils, etc.

Bibliography

Fiction

Christelow, Eileen. *Five Little Monkeys Jumping on the Bed.* Clarion Books, 1990.

Christelow, Eileen. *Five Little Monkeys Sitting in a Tree.* Clarion Books, 1993.

French, Jackie Koller. *One Monkey Too Many.* Harcourt Brace, 1999.

Gelman, Rita Golden. *More Spaghetti, I Say!* Cartwheel Books, 1993.

Perkins, Al. *Hand, Hand, Fingers, Thumb.* Random House, 1969.

Rey, Margaret and H. A. Rey. *The Complete Adventures of Curious George.* Hougton Mifflin Company, 1995.

Nonfiction

Albee, Sarah. *Very First Things to Know About Monkeys.* Workman Publishing Company, 1999.

Canizares, Susan and Pamela Chanko. *Monkeys.* Scholastic, 1998.

Fowler, Allan. *Monkeys Are a Lot Like Us.* Children's Press, 1996.

Hynes, Robert. *Amazing Monkeys.* National Geographic Society, 1999.

Pfloog, Jan. *The Monkey Book.* Golden Books, 1998.

Prunier, James. *Monkeys and Apes.* Scholastic, 1999.

Answer Key

Page 19

Sample answers are provided.
Accept all reasonable responses.

1. *Caps for Sale*
2. Esphyr Slobodkina
3. a man sleeping in a tree, monkeys hiding behind the tree, and a stack of caps.
4. Accept all reasonable responses.
5. The back of the book tells us that the book won the Lewis Carroll Shelf Award. It gives a brief summary.
6. 0–590–41080–6
7. Accept all reasonable answers related to identifying the specific book title and publisher.
8. *Caps for Sale: A Tale of a Peddler, Some Monkeys, and Their Monkey Business*; There is a subtitle listed on the title page.
9. Accept all reasonable revisions to predictions.
10. Scholastic, Inc.
11. 1940, 1947
12. The book is dedicated to Rosalind and Emmy Jean and to their grandfather.

Page 22

Sample responses are provided.
Accept all reasonable answers.

1. Once there was a peddler selling caps.
2. One day, he couldn't sell any caps.
3. So he sat down under a tree to nap.
4. When he woke up, all of his caps were gone but one.
5. He looked up in the tree and saw a monkey on every branch with a cap on its head.
6. The peddler didn't know what to do. He shook his finger, shook his hands, and stomped his feet.
7. The monkeys copied everything the peddler did.

8. Finally, the peddler took off his cap and threw it down.
9. The monkeys took off their caps and threw them down.
10. The peddler picked up the caps and began to sell them again.

Page 24

cannot	can't
could not	couldn't
I will	I'll
that is	that's
I am	I'm
will not	won't
have not	haven't

Page 25

1. peddler
2. peddler
3. monkeys
4. peddler
5. peddler
6. monkeys
7. peddler
8. monkeys

Page 26

Answers are not provided in the story. Questions are designed to have students critically think about aspects of the book. Answers will vary. Accept all reasonable answers.

Page 27

1. !
2. .
3. .
4. .
5. .
6. ?
7. . or !
8. .
9. .
10. .

Page 28

Sample answers are provided.
Accept all reasonable responses.

cap, tap, flap, sap
top, mop, cop, drop
like, Mike, bike, hike
blue, clue, shoe, moo
town, down, frown, brown
not, cot, dot, lot
red, head, said, fed
rest, nest, best, test
tree, bee, see, fee
sleep, beep, keep, leap
time, dime, lime, slime
hand, band, sand, land

Page 31

1. 17
2. 16
3. 4 gray, 4 brown, 4 blue, 4 red
4. $0.50
5. 0
6. 8
7. 8
8. 16
9. $8.00

Page 33

Accept all answers which add up to fifty cents.

Page 34

Students should glue the caps in the second row, fourth column.

Page 35

red, blue, red
brown, brown, blue
gray, blue, blue
gray, blue, red
brown, brown, blue
red, gray
brown

Page 37

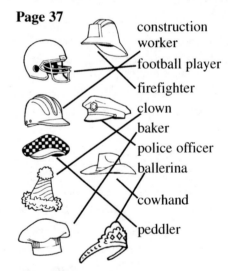

construction worker
football player
firefighter
clown
baker
police officer
ballerina
cowhand
peddler

Page 38

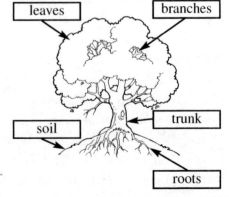

leaves
branches
soil
trunk
roots